Also by Jason M. Frazier

Fill in the Blank, Volume 1:
Inspiring Truths in a Busy World

Gravity

Gravity

The Weight
We Carry

Jason M. Frazier

Published by CreateSpace and Amazon.com
Printed in the United States of America

First Edition: October 2018

Edited by: Kimberly Townsend and Joshua Verkerk

Unless otherwise noted, Scripture quotations are taken from the New International Version of the Holy Bible available for free on www.BibleGateway.com.

Graphic design by Naomi Mesa

ISBN-13: 9781729295380

Dedications

To my Lord & Savior Jesus Christ:
As the lyrics of the worship song, "Jesus, All for Jesus" exclaim, I owe you "All I am and have and ever hope to be."

To my wife:
Thanks for being my biggest fan. Your feedback and support push me to be the best I can in every way.

To my children:
Being your dad is the greatest achievement ever. Watching you all grow has been wonderful and I have treasured every moment.

CONTENTS

ACKNOWLEDGMENTS

The original form of this book was a series of sermons preached at Friendship Church in Richmond, Texas. This church has been a loving and wonderful family to us, without whom this book would most likely not exist.

I am also incredibly grateful for my two editors, Kimberly Townsend and Joshua Verkerk. They provided much needed feedback on this book and helped me tremendously as a writer.

Introduction

Life is tough. Regardless of where you come from, what ethnicity you are, what socioeconomic level at which you live, or how many degrees you have earned, life is still tough. It will weigh you down with all sorts of burdens and difficulties.

We often think of burdens in a completely negative context. We think of the things that we carry on our shoulders as things of which we would gladly rid ourselves. Yet the reality is that some things that weigh on us are good things. Some burdens we gladly bear.

For instance, we gladly bear the weight of love. If you have ever been in a serious relationship, you understand that love is a burden. To love someone is a choice you make every single day. We willingly choose to bear this weight because we want to sustain a meaningful relationship with that person.

If you are a Christian, then you also bear the weight of the gospel which is the good news about Jesus Christ we are commanded to share with everyone on the planet. It is a burden, but it is *not* one of which we want to rid ourselves. We bear this burden in obedience to Christ's

Great Commission to His disciples found in five passages: Matthew 28:16-20, Mark 16:14-18, Luke 24:44-49, John 20:19-23, and Acts 1:4-8.

However, we recognize that there are some things weighing on us which we would love to shed. We bear the weight of regret, the weight of careless words, or the weight of silence when we should speak up. For some, these things weigh us down so significantly that they keep us from moving forward in our discipleship journey with Jesus Christ.

My hope is that, as you read these chapters, you learn which burdens to put on and which need to shed. As the gravity of being a fully-discipled follower of Jesus Christ weighs on you, I hope you see yourself through His eyes. I hope you know who you are in His identity. Ultimately, I hope that this book helps you to know Him more and to become more like Jesus.

1

The Weight of Words

Every year, many people make a New Year's resolution to get in better shape and shed some physical weight through the year. Folks are tired of their clothes not fitting right anymore. They are tired of being out of breath as they go up a flight of stairs. They realize that those nightly milkshakes might be adding up. I suggest that all of us could be in better shape spiritually as well–to shed the weight of things that are weighing us down spiritually.

So let's begin with this question: Have you ever said something that you immediately regretted? Of course, I already know the answer to that question before I asked it. We all have. Something came out of our mouths and we thought, "Well, that wasn't a good idea." If you're not sure… and you're married, just ask your spouse if you've ever done that. I think you already know the answer to that question, too.

During my college years, I would often visit my parents on the weekends. One weekend in particular, I felt that my mom was being a too passive-aggressive towards me. Thinking I was being funny, I said, "Pack your bags! We're going on a guilt trip!" The look of horror on her face said it all. I had wounded my sweet mother with my words. I've never forgotten that moment and how hurting her made me feel. It's a memory I would like to forget, I assure you. Yet I can't because it reinforced the lessons contained in this chapter.

Sometimes we might not remember the hurtful words we say because we weren't the one who was hurt by the words. However, we typically do remember the occasions when someone said carelessly spoken words that offended us. If you've ever wondered why that is the case, it's because our brains seem to be wired to remember moments attached with strong emotions a lot better. We tend to remember our happiest and saddest moments due to the significant emotions that accompany those memories.

To be honest, saying things I regret happens more often than I would like. I distinctly remember various times where I said something stupid to someone I cared about. Random movie quotes or jokes popped in my head and they were rarely the best source of appropriate replies. When I was in middle and high school, I had to be quick-witted with the comebacks. If someone insulted you, you had to one-up them or all your friends would make fun of you. I got really good at the insults.

The problem was that the venom that came out of my mouth never stopped. Insults became my defense mechanism to keep anyone from getting close enough to hurt me. I was funny and witty, and ultimately hurtful. If someone couldn't keep up, they would get their feelings hurt very easily and often.

Near the end of my time in high school, I got serious about my relationship with God, but my habit of insults was a hard one to break. It pushed people away and belittled them. I told myself that if people got offended, it was their problem due to their lack of humor.

One day, I said something particularly rude to a friend of mine. Tears welled up in her eyes and I knew I had crossed the line. I told another friend of mine that I hated acting that way and pushing all my friends away. It happened too often for me to continue ignoring.

I started to quote Psalm 141:3 in my prayers every day. It says: "Set a guard over my mouth, Lord; keep watch over the door of my lips."

Every. Single. Day. I made that Scripture my daily prayer.

When I felt myself about to say something rude and hurtful, I would literally put my hand over my mouth to stop myself. I realized that my words were having a profound effect on my relationships. I tried to guard myself from getting wounded by others, but in doing so I had wounded my friends in the process.

The Bible isn't silent on the issue of the weight of our words. Throughout its pages, God repeatedly gives us examples and instruction on the effect our words have. Here are some of the principles we find in the Bible on this subject.

First: *Words are either creative or destructive, so use them to create!* Several times in the Bible, God created with His words. He spoke something into existence that didn't exist before. Repeatedly in the first chapter of Genesis, God wanted to create something, so He spoke it forth, and it came into existence. At least nine times in the first chapter of Genesis, the author used the phrase "God said" to show how He created something.

Jesus did the same thing in Luke 18 with a blind beggar.

> As Jesus approached Jericho, a blind man was sitting by the roadside begging. When he heard the crowd going by, he asked what was happening. They told him, "Jesus of Nazareth is passing by." He called out, "Jesus, Son of David, have mercy on me!" Those who led the way rebuked him and told him to be quiet, but he shouted all the more, "Son of David, have mercy on me!" Jesus stopped and ordered the man to be brought to him. When he came near, Jesus asked him, "What do you want me to do for you?" "Lord, I want to see," he replied. Jesus said to him, "Receive your sight; your faith has healed you." Immediately he received his sight and followed Jesus, praising God. (Luke 18:35-43)

Jesus allowed the man's words to create a new reality for him. He was blind, Jesus asked him what he wanted to receive, the man said he wanted his sight, and Jesus said that the man's own faith had healed him. His faith had created a new reality for him in which to go forward.

Let me pause here to give a pastoral clarification. Please understand that any biblical principle can be taken to extremes and misinterpreted. However, extreme beliefs do not negate the truth of a biblical principle. The abuse of God's grace by some does not negate the truth of grace.

Some churches teach that you cannot lose your salvation which they call unconditional eternal security while other churches seem to teach unconditional eternal insecurity in that you can never really know if you are saved. Some churches teach that instruments are a part of biblical worship, while other churches teach that they are not because instruments were never mentioned in the New Testament. Some churches teach that speaking in tongues has ceased while other churches teach that the Pentecostal gifts are still as vibrant as ever.

When I was growing up in Pentecostal churches, the phrase "name it and claim it" was very popular. The principle was founded on scriptures that demonstrate that since God spoke things into existence, you can too…that God had given us the same ability to create and claim things as He possesses.

The problem is that there are a considerable number of people who have abused this concept, misinterpreted it, and took it to extremes. This caused the knee-jerk reaction in many Pentecostal churches to reject ever talking about biblical prosperity and to even belittle those who do talk about it.

I know it's a tender subject with some people because they have seen the abuses and how the world perceives the so-called "prosperity gospel." For instance, in the late 1980s, a pastor said that God told him he had to raise $8,000,000 for medical missionary teams to be sent out or God would "call him home."[1] God wasn't asking him to give that much, but for other people to give it to him. I think many rational people thought, "God threatened you with death if your fundraising campaign didn't succeed? That seems a *little* extreme."

So it's understandable that Christians can be very touchy on this issue. The truth is that God does want us to prosper and be blessed because He has promised that to those who are obedient to Him. Prosperity isn't about getting rich for the sake of being rich. Prosperity is about being "blessed to be a blessing" and God is all about that.

This concept leads into my next point: *Words determine our destination, so choose them wisely!* In his letter, James, who was the brother of Jesus, gave one of the best teachings on the power of our words. He used the analogy that when you put a bit and bridle on a horse, you can make that horse go anywhere you want. It makes the horse obey you and puts it into complete submission to you. He also used the analogy of the rudder on a boat. When you turn the rudder, it turns the ship. If you aren't going the direction you want to go, you turn the rudder the other way and you'll go in a different direction.

> Likewise, the tongue is a small part of the body, but it makes great boasts. Consider what a great forest is set on fire by a small spark. The tongue also is a fire, a world of evil among the parts of the body. It corrupts the whole body, sets the whole course of one's life on fire, and is itself set on fire by hell. All kinds of animals, birds, reptiles, and sea creatures are being tamed and have been tamed by mankind, but no human being can tame the tongue. It is a restless evil, full of deadly poison. With the tongue we praise our Lord and Father, and with it we curse human beings, who have been made in God's likeness. Out of the same mouth come praise and cursing. My

brothers and sisters, this should not be. (James 3:5-10)

Since our tongue is like the rudder on a boat, our words have the ability to determine our destination. If you're a negative person, you will see the negative in every situation. It doesn't matter what it is, pessimists always find something to complain about.

People who are filled with negativity have the motto: aim low and you're never disappointed. But that seems like a pretty miserable way to live. If you're a positive person, however, you see the silver lining in every situation. Abraham Lincoln is credited with saying, "We can complain that rose bushes have thorns, or rejoice because thorn bushes have roses."

Optimists drive pessimists crazy. I think optimism is just the better way to live. Yes, I can complain about my situation, but all my complaining does is increase my stress level, increase my blood pressure, and decrease my happiness and joy. By complaining, not a single thing about my situation has changed.

Instead of allowing my words to take me to a destination of negativity and frustration, I want them to take me to a place of peace and assurance that God's got it under control. Jesus reminded us that it's our faith in God that shapes our reality.

In Matthew 17, the disciples tried to cast out a demon from a little boy, but they weren't able. Jesus walked up, rebuked the demon, and the boy was healed immediately. Matthew 17:19-20 says:

> Then the disciples came to Jesus in private and asked, "Why couldn't we drive it out?" He replied, "Because you have so little faith. Truly I tell you, if you have faith as small as a mustard seed, you can say to this mountain, 'Move from here to there,' and it will move. Nothing will be impossible for you."

Sometimes people get hung up on whether Jesus was exaggerating–nobody has ever seen a mountain move from one point to the another point just by saying it. When that becomes the focus, people really miss His point. Jesus was saying that you determine how big your obstacles are by your viewpoint. If you worry, then your obstacles will be huge and God will look small. You won't have the faith to overcome them.

If you know God is in control, your obstacles will look small and God will be huge. You will have the faith to determine whether those mountains and obstacles in your way become stumbling blocks or stepping stones in your walk with God. Words determine your destination, so choose them wisely.

Third: *Words are either encouraging or discouraging, so use them to encourage!* If you've ever endured verbal abuse, then you know the power of words to tear you down. Discouraging and insulting words ring in your ear for days and weeks after they were spoken. You can look in the mirror and hear words spoken over you years before. Some people never get past them.

In the first few chapters of Deuteronomy, God told Moses to commission Joshua to take over the leadership. Twice in those chapters, God told Moses to encourage Joshua and strengthen him with his words. Why? Because the task ahead of him was difficult and discouraging. God wanted the words of Moses to ring in Joshua's ears when he felt like quitting. In Judges 20, the Israelites encouraged each other with their words after they had a serious military defeat. They strengthened the heart and will of each other so they wouldn't give up.

Paul commanded the church in 1 Thessalonians 5:11, "Therefore encourage one another and build each other up…" The word for "encourage" here is the same word Jesus used for the Holy Spirit when He called Him the "Comforter." It means to come alongside and to strengthen. God has not called Christians to criticize one another but to encourage, comfort, and strengthen one another. None of us can succeed in the spiritual warfare we go through by ourselves. We need each other; we need to lift each other up, pray for each other, and speak life, blessing, and encouragement into each other.

The Scripture I shared earlier from James 3 reminds us that we have the power of life and death in the words we say. We can build up or we can tear down. We can create, dream, and breathe life into people with our words. Or we can destroy, discourage, and tear down. Ephesians 4:29 says, "Do not let any unwholesome talk come out of your mouths, but only what is helpful for building others up according to their needs, that it may benefit those who listen."

I'm sure most of you had mothers that reminded you, "If you don't have something nice to say, don't say anything at all." Honestly, that's really good advice. Our words have tremendous power to encourage or discourage someone. Typically the people we would say such things to are loved ones, and we don't want to tear them down.

Our words essentially turn people into *square watermelons*. I know that statement seems completely random, but it's really profound once you understand what I mean. In Japan, farmers take small watermelons and place them into a square metal box. As it grows, the watermelon fills up the container to become a square. After the farmers take it out of the box, it never changes shape. It stays a square because it was forced to be that way.

Our words have the exact same effect. If a person hears enough times that they are stupid, fat, or ugly, they will believe it regardless of the reality. Just like the watermelon stays in the shape of a square when it's let out of the box, even after a person is out of that abusive situation, they will continue to believe what was spoken about them.

The American poet Shaun Shane said, "If only our tongues were made of glass, how much more careful we would be when we speak." Dwell on that statement for a minute. Read it again if you need to.

If you were a victim of verbal abuse, don't allow that to be passed down to another generation. Break the cycle of abuse by making it a matter of prayer. Give God control over your words.

I believe God wants to heal His people from the wounds of careless and hurtful words. Maybe you lost control of your words and you said some terrible things. As you honestly reflect on your life, you know you need God's forgiveness and help to stop the cycle. Some of you need to get control over what comes out of your mouth. To do so, you need to gain control over the source.

Jesus said in Luke 6:45 that what comes out of your mouth is just the overflow of what's in your heart. If evil, nasty, and hurtful things come out of your mouth, you have a heart issue.

It's time to let God heal your heart so that he can fix what comes out of your mouth.

Maybe you were a victim of abuse, and you have carried the weight of it all your life, but now you are ready to be free. You have lived with the decrees of abusive people hanging over your head, telling you they think who you are. As you read the scriptures in which God calls you his son or daughter, as He gives you authority, and as he delights over you, you have always struggled with finding your identity in Christ.

If that is you, if you need forgiveness or healing, I wholeheartedly believe that you can be free from this weight–this burden that's crushing your spirit and declaring a limited and false identity. It's time for you to be free and to see yourself through God's eyes.

Before you turn to the next chapter, would you bc willing to pray about this issue? Would you simply ask God for forgiveness if your words have wounded others and pursue reconciliation with that person? Or would you ask God for healing in your heart from the wounding words of others? I believe God *can* and *will* heal you. I believe God wants the words of our mouth to build others up and not tear them down.

It starts with *me*.
It starts with *you*.
And it starts *now*.

2

The Weight of the Gospel

I'm a Christian because I heard the gospel and accepted Jesus Christ as my Lord and Savior. I'm a Protestant because I don't belong to the Roman Catholic Church, but rather to a group formed out of one which protested five hundred years ago.

I'm Evangelical because I believe God has called all of us to evangelize – to share the gospel with people who have never heard it. I'm Pentecostal because I believe the Holy Spirit gives Christians power to be effective witnesses in sharing the gospel as Jesus declared in Acts 1:8.

You may hear the word "gospel" used a lot at church, but sometimes people struggle with understanding what that word means. People use it to describe various church things. You can have a "Gospel Singing" at your church. You can listen to Southern Gospel music. You can go to a church called Gospel Tabernacle. My dad used to call fried chicken, the "Gospel bird" because we ate it every other Sunday after church.

What does the word actually mean? Simply put, "gospel" means "good news." Specifically, it refers to the good news that Jesus Christ was born on this earth, died for our sins, was resurrected, and ascended into heaven. The good news is that our God's not dead; He's very alive! That's the gospel. It really doesn't have anything to do with a music style, a preaching style, or a deep-fried chicken. It's the message that Christians must proclaim to the world so that the world can be saved.

The first thing to know about the gospel is: *The gospel is eternal.* Did you know that every religious leader, of every single religion, died and was buried? Moses died. The Virgin Mary died. Muhammad died. Buddha died. All of the founders of Hinduism died. Joseph Smith died. L. Ron Hubbard died.

Our religious leader, Jesus, also died and was buried. But the gospel–the good news–was that God brought Him back to life on the third day. His grave is the only grave that lies empty! On the third day after His death, His funeral clothes weren't wrapped around a body anymore. The stone had been rolled away. More than five hundred people saw Jesus walking around–fully alive–after He had been crucified and resurrected. These people were willing to go to their deaths rather than recant their testimony about the risen Lord.

Jesus had such a profound impact on recorded history that it was split in two: B.C. and A.D.–Before Christ and *anno Domini* (a Latin phrase meaning *in the year of our Lord*). Even for those politically-correct folk that use BCE (Before the Common Era) and CE (Common Era), the moment that splits those two designators is still Christ's birth. Call it what you will, the fact remains that the gospel of Jesus Christ changed humanity and history forever.

The message of Jesus Christ won't be watered down, diluted, or destroyed. The gospel is eternal and it will go on for another two thousand years until the Lord says, "Son, go get your Bride." The good news of Jesus Christ is eternal, never ending, and never failing.

Paul wrote in 2 Corinthians 3:18, "And we all, who with unveiled faces contemplate the Lord's glory, are being transformed into his image with ever-increasing glory, which comes from the Lord, who is the Spirit." The word transformed here is the Greek word *metamorphosis*. It means to change, to transfigure, or to turn into something new.

The next thing you should know about the gospel is this: *The gospel is transformational.* Like a caterpillar which transforms into a butterfly, the gospel transforms us who were dead in our trespasses and sins to be fully alive in Jesus Christ. Two thousand years ago, it transformed fishermen and farmers into faith-filled followers of Jesus.

Following Christ did something to them that made them into new creatures. It gave them a way to encounter God. It gave them access. They no longer had to go through an earthly priest to have their sins forgiven or their prayers heard. They had immediate and permanent access to God through Jesus.

Therefore, since we have a great high priest who has ascended into heaven, Jesus the Son of God, let us hold firmly to the faith we profess. For we do not have a high priest who is unable to empathize with our weaknesses, but we have one who has been tempted in every way, just as we are – yet he did not sin. Let us then approach God's throne of grace with confidence, so that we may receive mercy and find grace to help us in our time of need. (Hebrews 4:14-16)

The transformational element of the gospel established a new purpose for their lives. Their lives weren't to be lived for selfish causes. Instead, they believed that their sole purpose in life was to spread the gospel of Jesus Christ all over the world.

Their encounter with God had convinced them that their lives were not their own; they had been bought with a price and would spend the rest of their lives travelling all over the world to preach this gospel of Jesus. The gospel transformed these men and women who became the Early Church and it still has the power to transform us.

The gospel is universal; it's for everyone. We know that not everyone is saved because they choose not to accept the gospel, but salvation is available for everyone. John 3:16 says, "For God so loved the world that he gave his one and only Son, that whoever believes in him shall not perish but have eternal life."

God's love for humanity was so amazing that He gave up the most precious thing in the whole universe to be tormented and crucified so that He became our once-and-for-all sacrifice. If we are willing to accept that sacrifice as our own, we won't perish, but live in God's eternal salvation.

Every person on the planet is entitled to hear the gospel. It's our job to arrange that meeting. We carry the gospel message everywhere we go. The word "Christian" was first spoken in the city of Antioch as an insult. They were frustrated with all these Christians, do-gooders, all these "little Christs" walking around the city. However, the early Christians took this insult as a compliment and we have gladly been referred to by the name ever since. Our job as "little Christs" is to take this gospel to whatever part of the world God takes us.

Jesus was asked by his disciples for some signs that the end of days was near. In Matthew 24, Jesus said there would be wars, rumors of wars, famines, earthquakes, a great persecution of Christians, heresy filling the churches, backsliding, false prophets, and an increase of wickedness and selfishness in the world. Then in Matthew 24:14, Jesus said, "And this gospel of the kingdom will be preached in the whole world as a testimony to all nations, and then the end will come."

This gospel, this message about Jesus, must be and will be preached before the end of the earth. This means that we need to be busy proclaiming the gospel and getting it out to all of humanity. Peter spoke about the end times in 2 Peter 3:11-12 which says, "Since everything will be destroyed that way, what kind of people ought you to be? You ought to live holy and godly lives as you look forward to the day of God and *speed its coming*" (emphasis mine). This verse means that we can hasten or speed up Christ's return if we get busy doing the one thing that holds it back: preaching the gospel so that it is heard by every person.

Since salvation is only through the good news about Jesus, the message of his life, death, and resurrection has to be shared with the whole world. This is why Jesus gave us the Great Commission. In Matthew 28:19, Jesus said, "Therefore go and make disciples of all nations..." Mark's version of it is slightly different. Mark 16:15 says, "Go into all the world and preach the gospel to all creation."

If you remember your early years in English class, there are three main sentence types. Declarative sentences state a fact or opinion: "I have an apple." Interrogatories ask a question: "Do you have an apple?" Imperatives give a command: "Go get me an apple!" However, some English-speaking cultures combine sentence types by saying, "Go get me an apple, if you please?"

This hybrid sentence type is the way some Christians choose to interpret the Great Commission. "Go and proclaim the gospel…if you feel up to it, if you would like to, if it's not too much trouble, if isn't too much of an imposition, if you don't have anything better to do." It is *not* the Great Suggestion or the Great Opinion. It is the Great Commission which, for Christians, is really a Great Commandment. We have been given a directive on how to occupy our time.

Some of you might feel like you are exactly where God wants you to be and going overseas would be out of God's will for you. And you would probably be right. When Jesus said, "Go into all the world and preach the gospel…" you understand that you live and work in the part of the world to which God has called you.

Some of you are those who fund ministry rather than act as the face of ministry. Paul said in 1 Corinthians 12 that each member of the body has different jobs. Some are the mouthpieces that speak the word, some are the eyes that see needs, some are the ears that listen for the cries of the hurting, some are the hands that give to ministry, and some are the feet that go to where the needs are.

Every one of those parts is necessary for the body to function in perfect health. While you may not be called to move abroad and become a missionary, you absolutely can be the support system for them through your finances, in your prayers, by putting together care packages, or in taking short-term trips overseas to work alongside missionaries.

While God may not have called you to go overseas, you are, however, still called to minister where you are. Jesus said in Acts 1:8, "But you will receive power when the Holy Spirit comes on you; and you will be my witnesses in Jerusalem, and in all Judea and Samaria, and to the ends of the earth."

The question you need to answer is: *What is my Jerusalem?* In what area or community am I in everyday where I can be a witness? Where can I can obey the Great Commission by being a living testimony of God's grace and salvation? I will support those that go, but I will also be faithful here where God has placed me!

Consider this question: *What is the gospel worth to you?* Has Jesus changed you so much that He's worth everything to you? If God asked for you to sacrifice something for Him, is there anything you would withhold from Him?

Would you rather have money than Jesus? Would you rather have your health than Jesus? Would you rather be skinny and have six-pack abs than Jesus? Would you rather have 300 cable channels than Jesus? Would you rather have two dozen Christmas presents under the tree than Jesus?

Those might seem like ridiculous questions, but here is why I ask them: As I'm writing this, there are around 250 million Americans age 18 or older. What do those 250 million people spend their money on each year? According to some sources on the Internet, they spend $700 billion dollars on Christmas presents. They spend $57.7 billion on cable TV subscriptions, $45 billion on diet programs, $21 billion at Starbucks, $13.7 billion on Netflix, and $8.4 billion on Halloween candy.

By contrast, they give $2.5 billion to missions. Of that $2.5 billion, $450 million is given for the Gospel to be brought to unreached people groups. In 2016, Americans spent as much money on getting the gospel to unreached people as they did on costumes *for their pets* at Halloween.[1] Let that sink in for a minute.

This should concern us that as Americans, missions–preaching the gospel to the world–is not as high of a priority as Halloween pet costumes, Netflix, Starbucks, gym memberships, or Christmas presents. *This isn't a trivial matter!* This is eternal salvation for those who have never heard the gospel. It's literally a matter of eternal life and death for these people.

For every dollar given to the average Protestant church, 2 cents goes to missions. This means that the average church gives 2% of its income to missions. I've pastored churches that have averaged giving 5%, 7%, and sometimes even 11% of their annual church income to missions. While that's much better than the national average, I can't escape the question: *is that good enough?*

I challenge you, dear reader, to look at your giving statements and see how much you gave to missions last year. For the next several days, I want you to prayerfully ask the Lord to help you give more. This isn't about getting a plaque on the wall or the church receiving recognition about how much we give to missions. This is about getting the gospel around the world and seeing people saved as a result. *This is an emergency!* If it were your son or daughter, is there any luxury expense that you would hold onto rather than ensure their salvation?

You might wonder why this is so important. Why should you give sacrificially, above your tithes and offerings, to missions? Jesus said the greatest commandment is to love the Lord your God with everything you have. It's living a life of love to God where He is your priority. God so loved the world that He gave. We should love Him wholeheartedly as well. This commandment can be summed up in one word: *worship*. Then Jesus said: the second greatest commandment is just like it, "Love your neighbor as yourself." What better way to love our neighbors than to share the gospel with them?

If the greatest commandment is worship, then the second greatest commandment is missions. Worship for those in relationship with God and missions for those who are not. If missions is the second greatest commandment of all of God's commands, then *what in the world are we doing spending more money on Starbucks and Netflix than we are on missions?* I challenge you to do the math in your personal finances and ask God what you can cut out. Then reinvest that money into missions.

We bear the weight of the gospel on our shoulders. Jesus said the gospel will be preached and then He told us as His disciples to go into the world and preach it! The gospel should be a heavy and welcome burden that motivates us to share the gospel with those around us and support the efforts of those who go where we cannot.

In Ezekiel 33, God appointed the prophet as a watchman for Israel. God said: When you see calamity coming, warn the people. If they hear the warning, do nothing about it, and destruction overtakes them, you are free from any guilt because you warned them. You told them it was going to happen. You offered them a path to salvation from the destruction to come. God told Ezekiel that when destruction came He will hold him accountable for their blood.

I believe that we are the modern-day watchmen on the walls. We have read the book. We know what is going to happen if people do not accept Jesus as their Savior. We cannot be silent. We cannot be distracted. We cannot have any higher priorities than worshiping God and making Him known among the nations.

If we are obedient and have done everything we can to warn people, then we will have faithfully shouldered the weight of the gospel. If we value our own comfort and entertainment more than we value the salvation of the lost, I firmly believe God will judge us for that.

I would rather God say, "Well done thy good and faithful servant. You were faithful in the things I put you in charge of. Come and enter into your master's happiness" than for Him to say, "You could have done so much more. I put so many people in your path for you to share the gospel with. I entrusted so much money for you to invest in the kingdom and support missions. So many more people could be in heaven right now if you had been faithful." To hear that from my Lord's lips would break my heart!

Every year, we want God to do more than we did the year before in our church and in our lives. We want to give more, go more, do more, reach more, and go deeper with God than ever before. Our world is lost and dying, and we are the light in this darkness. We are the only gospel that some people will ever see, so we have to be filled with God's love so they see Jesus in us.

I want you to make this your prayer: "What can I do to reach the lost? God, open my eyes to those around me and give me the boldness to share the gospel with them. Is there something I need to give up that's taking money away from me giving to missions? Is there anything in my life, Lord, that I'm treating as more important than you?" I challenge you to pray today about this issue and ask God to shine a light on your heart to see if there's anything that needs to change.

3

The Weight of Regret

At the time of this writing, I have three teenagers and twin eighteen-month-old babies. Therefore, I feel confident enough with my parenting experiences to say that I've learned the most valuable lesson in parenting: *how to keep your children alive.* That's really the major responsibility when children are young. Kids get into all sorts of things, they try to do dangerous activities, and they constantly test the limits. As a parent, you know the dangers involved in various activities and the worst-case scenarios. Your radar is always on to determine if any given situation could harm your child.

I grew up in an era where children didn't sit in car seats resembling NASCAR safety harnesses. We sat up front in the family station wagon. Being "buckled in" meant that your mom was holding onto you as she sat in the front seat. Kids played outside and shot each other with BB guns with no eye protection. Kids played with old-school Easy Bake ovens that would never pass safety regulations today.

"Here's a loaded gun and a fire hazard, kid. Go crazy." And we did!

We took as much medicine as we wanted from pill bottles because there was no such thing as child-proofed lids. Kids did a lot of dangerous things just to see what would happen. Questionable meats and cheeses were given to children. "Don't think of it as moldy bread; think of it as a preventative dose of penicillin."

Honestly, it's a wonder any of us survived. But we did! We survived without being covered in bubble wrap, having "safe spaces" or being strapped in the car like an astronaut when mom was just driving down the street to the store.

There was a new father who was proud of the bond he had with his daughter. She was over a year old and was already a daredevil. She loved to be tossed up in the air. In their house, it wasn't a problem. They had high ceilings and the father was very careful to never drop her.

However, one day the father and daughter were visiting his brother. His brother had just bought a house and wanted everyone to come over to check it out. While they were there, this new dad decided to show off the trick of tossing the little girl up in the air to show everyone how much she loved it.

Yet as the little girl left the safety of her father's arms and began soaring into the air, the look on the father's face changed rapidly. He immediately noticed that the room they were in didn't have the high ceilings to which he was accustomed...and there was a ceiling fan in the room...and the ceiling fan was on.

Gravity eventually took over and brought the little girl back into the safe and secure arms of her father, but not completely unscathed. The little girl was confused... and maybe a little concussed. She had never been hit upside the head by a ceiling fan before. It was a new experience for her. To keep the little girl from crying, he smiled at her, pulled her head in close to his chest–mainly checking for skull fractures–and assured her that she had done so well.

He kept an eye on the little girl for a few days to see if she was walking a little wobbly or talking to the walls, but all was well! There was no permanent damage and she acted as though it had never even happened...possibly because the head trauma kept her from remembering details. Needless to say, it taught the father a valuable lesson.

We have all done things we regret! Sometimes, things seemed really good at the time. It is only until after the action is committed that the person realizes, "That was definitely not a good idea."

In 1 Kings 12, we see an example of this from the Bible. When King Solomon died, his son, Rehoboam became King in his place. This new King is the grandson of King David–the man who was an amazing worshiper, leader, and who had such a humble and tender heart– and you just hope that this spiritual upbringing is enough to help Rehoboam make good choices. But in 1 Kings 12:1-16, it recounts a sad story of this foolish young man.

When Rehoboam ignored the advice of his father's counselors and heeded the advice of his friends, he set in motion a course of events which split Israel in two, creating the northern and southern kingdoms. Rehoboam's act of defiance where he refused to listen to good counsel caused ten tribes of Israel to rebel against him and set up their own King and kingdom.

At the time, Rehoboam never thought that would happen. He was Solomon's son, David's grandson. He was just flexing his muscles a little bit and he thought they would fall in line under his authority. They would never rebel. But they did and almost ninety percent of the tribes of his kingdom departed overnight.

Once reality set in, I'm sure it didn't take long for Rehoboam to regret what he had done. Regret is a powerful force in our lives. It brings to mind the phrase, "You can't unscramble an egg." God had told the prophets that this national division would take place, so there was no stopping it. This was one egg that Rehoboam could not unscramble.

There are some things we do in life that cannot be undone. A wound that cuts so deep that it never seems to heal; a breach of trust so painful that, even if the relationship is restored, those involved are filled with regret over what happened. But what can we do to make sure regret does not paralyze our lives and our walk with God?

The first thing is: *Listen to wisdom.* Wisdom comes in all forms. God can speak to us through the Bible. God can speak to us through other godly people who've been in similar situations. God can speak to us through the Holy Spirit, cautioning us not to do something we want to do or prompting us to do something on which we're hesitating.

Throughout the book of Proverbs, the aspect of wisdom is emphasized. Specifically in Proverbs 2:6, it says, "For the Lord gives wisdom; from his mouth come knowledge and understanding."

There's no greater source of wisdom than God. He knows the beginning and the end. He can see much further down the road than us. If we're willing to listen to His voice and obey it, we will always make the right decision.

I don't want to make a mistake and God doesn't want us to make mistakes either. He doesn't want to have to bail us out because we messed up. So one way to live without regret is to listen to wisdom and obey God when He speaks.

In 1994, I had just graduated from high school and was going to Bible college. I intended on studying pastoral ministry because I wanted to be a pastor like my dad. When I got there though, the Holy Spirit began dealing with me. I didn't know what God wanted me to study, only that He did not want me to major in pastoral ministry.

I was standing in line waiting to go through the registration process and was praying the whole time. "God, what do you want me to do? I thought you wanted me to study pastoral ministry. I feel like you have called me to be a pastor, but now I don't know what to do."

The Lord spoke right back to me and said, "Listen. Just listen." Suddenly, one of the administrators stuck his head out of the room where all the advisors were and yelled, "Urban ministry! Anyone for urban ministry?" The Lord immediately spoke to me, "Go!"

I went in, not having a clue what urban ministry was, what I would learn, or the course it would set for my life. In those days, urban ministry focused on church planting, outreach, and urban evangelism. Honestly, it's hard to get a full-time job at a church right out of college with that kind of a degree. For four years at Bible college, I didn't understand why

God told me to focus on that field of study, but I've never regretted it.

Since graduating, I've planted one church, I've been part of two church plant teams, and I've pastored one church revitalization–that's where an older church with a small group of people needs a new pastor to rebrand, restart, and grow the church to become a sovereign assembly. I wholeheartedly believe that listening to God's wisdom back in August 1994 prepared me for the path that He had put ahead of me. If you want to avoid regret, listen to wisdom.

Another way to avoid a life of regret is: *Learn from the mistakes of others.* I don't want to make the same mistakes as everyone else. I want to make all new ones! I write that jokingly, but it's often been said that we learn more from our failures than we do from our successes. I'm not afraid of failing; I'm afraid of not learning from that failure. Any chance I get, I talk to others and see what went wrong for them. What did they do incorrectly that may serve as a cautionary tale for me?

Paul wrote in Philippians 4:9, "Whatever you have learned or received or heard from me, or seen in me – put into practice. And the God of peace will be with you." Paul was far from perfect. He lost his temper, was impatient, and in my opinion, showed a little bit of arrogance at times in his letters. Yet his desire was to be like Jesus as he allowed the Spirit to purge the evil things in his life so he could resemble Jesus more and more. He wanted to pass on his life lessons to others so that they would not make the same mistakes as him.

If you have children, do them a tremendous blessing by teaching them to avoid the mistakes you made. Teach them the situations to avoid, the people to avoid, and the predispositions to certain sins to avoid. Give them the worst-case scenarios because it's better for them to know that and be able to avoid it, than for them to become one of those worst-case scenarios.

Also: *Be slow to speak.* One thing our modern age isn't short on is opinions. People have opinions about everything! On Facebook, I was added to a group of people in my town where they talk about different local restaurants. I like hearing the recommendations of places to try. It's helpful when I'm trying to decide on where to go for date night. But when somebody finds a place they do not like, *good gravy* they can be brutal in their reviews.

There was a new donut shop that was repeatedly slammed by people who don't like their donuts. The shop has said, "We had a few hiccups in our first week. But we're sorting it out. Please be patient with us." Nope! These people treat restaurants the way they treat parachutes: if you didn't work out for me once, you won't work for me ever again!

We might think, "There's nothing wrong with sharing our opinions," and that's true. But there's a right way and a wrong way to do it. Insulting, belittling, or slandering someone isn't sharing your opinion. It is rude and unnecessary. Take it from someone who used to say whatever rude thing popped into his head: you won't have any friends left at the end of the day if you don't learn how to speak tactfully and respectfully.

In James 1:19-20, he wrote, "My dear brothers and sisters, take note of this: Everyone should be quick to listen, slow to speak, and slow to become angry, because human anger does not produce the righteousness that God desires."

Many times, we live out this scripture completely backwards. Instead of being quick to listen, slow to speak, and slow to become angry–we are slow to listen, quick to speak, and quick to become angry. What happens then? It produces human anger which leads to actions we will end up regretting. Absolutely nothing good comes from opening your mouth in anger. You will end up saying something you can never take back and something that person can never unhear.

If you struggle with this area specifically, go back and read the chapter on "The Weight of Words." I think it will give you some good, biblical guidance for guarding your words to prevent them from wounding someone and allowing others words to wound you. If you want to avoid a lot of regret, be slow to speak.

Another way to avoid living in regret is: *Don't be tempted by what-ifs.* Sometimes nostalgia overtakes our common sense and we long to go back to the "good ole days." We thumb through our old yearbooks and ask ourselves, "I wonder what life would have been like if I had dated that person. What if I had moved there? What if I had gone to a different college? What if I had chosen a different field of work? What would my life look like?"

We start to allow those "what-ifs" to become fantasies that our life would be better in the present had we gone down a different path in the past. However, I believe that hardly anything about your life would be different–at least not for the better–because it's still you on that path. It's still your personality, your struggles, and your sins. If you're a Christian and you yielded your life to Christ, then unless He has told you that you are out of His will, then you are right where He wants you to be. All those "what-ifs" serve only to tempt you to get out of God's will and into your own.

You might be going through difficulty or your marriage might be really struggling right now, and you ask, "God wanted this for me?" No, of course he doesn't want you to suffer or struggle. That's typically a result of selfishness rearing its ugly head in a relationship. If your spouse is being selfish, then pray for God to help them. There's no better way to show God's grace and mercy than when we are patient, gracious, and forgiving with someone who may not deserve it. You know...the way God does with us.

I know that every situation is different and I need to make myself completely clear here. I am absolutely not saying that a person should stay in a situation if there is abuse. But apart from that situation, if we find ourselves looking for an exit because the situation doesn't look like we would like it to–whether that's at a job, a family relationship, a marriage, or wherever– we have to go to God's word in these situations. Thankfully, Paul gives us guidance on this in the book of Romans.

He wrote in Romans 5:2-4, "...And we boast in the hope of the glory of God. Not only so, but we also glory in our sufferings, because we know that suffering produces perseverance; perseverance, character; and character, hope." If we know we are where God wants us, listen to God's wisdom before making any decision that you may come to regret. Don't let yourself be constantly enamored with thoughts of "what-if" and think that your life would be better. Any other path is out of God's will for us and that automatically makes it worse.

Thus far, we have exclusively addressed how to avoid living in regret based on our actions. But with all the bedside visitation I've done in over 20 years of ministry, do you know that most people don't regret actions they took? They regret inactions–the things they wanted to do and never did.

In my ministry, I've never once heard a dying person turn to their family and say, "You know, I wish I had spent more time at the office. Yes, I wish I had really worked harder on that report for my boss. I wish I had worked more off the clock and skipped a few more family dinners to get that big promotion."

What I *have* heard is a helpless person realizing that the most meaningful way they could have spent their time was wasted. They say things like, "I wish I had spent more time with my family. If only I hadn't worked so much, I could've saved my marriage. If I had only spent more time with my kids, they would have known how much I cared about them." On and on they go. These sweet, dying people open their mouths and out pours a lifetime of regret about what they should have done instead.

If you want to avoid the weight of regret: *Don't live your life in the rear-view mirror.* Mark Batterson is the pastor of an Assembly of

God church in Washington D.C. and he wrote a book called *In a Pit with a Lion on a Snowy Day*. It's an odd choice of title, but it's based on an easily over-looked passage in 2 Samuel 23:20-21:

> Benaiah son of Jehoiada, a valiant fighter from Kabzeel, performed great exploits. He struck down Moab's two mightiest warriors. He also went down into a pit on a snowy day and killed a lion. And he struck down a huge Egyptian. Although the Egyptian had a spear in his hand, Benaiah went against him with a club. He snatched the spear from the Egyptian's hand and killed him with his own spear.

The main point of his book–which I recommend–is that at the end of your life, you will regret more the things you didn't do rather than the things you did.

Oskar Schindler risked his life to provide a list of 1,097 names of Jews which he saved from Nazi concentration camps. Though he spent his entire fortune doing so and died completely broke, there are over 6,000 descendants of the Schindler Jews alive today.

He never regretted his life-saving action; his chief regret was not saving more people.

The Bible we read chronicles God working through the lives of people who were willing to be risk takers. People who were willing to face down giants, lions, and wicked leaders of their day. Abraham, Isaac, Jacob, Moses, Joshua, Gideon, Deborah, Samuel, David, Ruth, Esther, Nehemiah, Daniel, Mary, Peter, Paul, and countless others faced impossible situations, took risks for God, and reaped rewards beyond anything they could have imagined. If you feel God is telling you to step out and believe Him to do the impossible, you've got plenty of examples of people who did the same thing and saw God do the miraculous.

This is only possible if we focus on the last thing that will help us avoid regret: *Make Jesus the center of your life.* If we say we are Christians but Jesus is not at the center of our lives, then are we *really* Christians? If obeying Jesus's commands and living the way He showed us to live is not really something we want to do, then are we *really* Christians? If we're content with coming to church once a week to get a spiritual pat on the back but ultimately living our life our way, then are we *really* Christians?

The truth is this: Christianity isn't a pleasure cruise; it's a battleship. We're sailing around in enemy territory, taking back enemy positions, rescuing people that the enemy has stolen, and waging war against the powers of darkness. I assure you, you're not going to do any of that on a Carnival cruise! We're at war with this present darkness (See Ephesians 6:12). We need to get things right with God and get to our battle stations.

Some Christians approach this spiritual walk with God like looking for a deck chair by the pool on a naval destroyer. *There ain't no deck chairs because there ain't no pool!* This is a wartime vessel because we have a very active and persistent enemy. 1 Peter 5:8 says, "Be alert and of sober mind. Your enemy the devil prowls around like a roaring lion looking for someone to devour."

The greatest comfort in that verse is this: the devil is a *roaring* lion. He's not a *devouring* lion. His teeth got pulled at Calvary. All he can do to us is make a whole lot of noise. He can roar! He can prowl around! He can get angry! But he is a toothless foe. Get your mind, your ears, and your eyes off of what the devil is doing, and fix your eyes on Jesus, the author and perfecter of your faith.

Jesus doesn't want us to be paralyzed with regret. He longs for us to be centered in His will, doing what He has called us to do, and living in right relationship with Him. If we listen to God's wisdom, if we learn from the mistakes of others, if are slow to speak, if we don't allow ourselves to be tempted by the what ifs of life, if we refuse to live our lives in the rear-view mirror, and if we make Jesus the center of it all, we will be well on our way to living our life *looking forward in anticipation* of God's work instead of *looking backwards in regret.*

If this message has resonated with you, before you do anything else, would you ask God to help you free yourself from any weight of regret? That might be due to actions you've done that you regret. Or it could be actions you should have done and didn't. I believe God will give you forgiveness for your mistakes and grace to get you back on the path where Jesus is at the center of your life.

4

The Weight of Glory

When I was about 20, I was asked to speak at a youth rally. I wanted to hear from God. I wanted to be walking in the spirit in a more powerful way. So I committed to fast all meals for a week. I had never done that, but I wanted so desperately to be closer to God than ever before.

All week long, I fasted and prayed. I prayed for God to speak to me so I would know what to share to these teenagers. I prayed that God would anoint me in a powerful way. I prayed that God would use me to impact these kids. Before the youth rally that weekend, I walked around the sanctuary and prayed. I felt more spiritual power in those moments that I had ever felt. Then I saw something that took my breath away.

Jesus appeared right before me. I was stunned. I fell completely silent. I looked deep into the image before me, but it was as if I was looking at Him like an old photography negative. I couldn't see color or definition of His face, but I could see glory and light all around Him. It was like I was looking into the face of the sun.

That moment changed me. Christianity was something that I had previously experienced through my parents. This moment in time was an experience that was just for me. The muscles in my stomach began to convulse, but not in a painful or uncomfortable way. It was a strong twitching that caused me to bend over. God's glory was all around me and it was pushing me to the floor. It was pushing me to be on my face before the Living God.

The word for "glory" in Hebrew is the word *kabod*. It means honor, splendor, reverence, and abundance. But the root word for *kabod* means "heaviness." God's glory was coming over me and it was quite literally pushing me gently to the floor. His heaviness was weighing on me and the only proper position to be in– when you're in the presence of God–is on your face. I wasn't afraid, I wasn't nervous, and I wasn't in pain. I wept in awe because I had been face-to-face with my Savior and I couldn't stand in his presence.

This leads to my first point when talking about the "weight of glory." *God's glory declares our position.* God doesn't exist to bring us glory; we exist to bring Him glory. We are nothing without Jesus. Yes, you can go awhile in your own strength; you can go awhile in your own talent; you can go awhile in your own resources. Yet you will never accomplish all that God has for you if you do it all on your own.

We are His children. He loves us and gives us spiritual gifts. But we have none of that if we're not submissive to our position in Christ. John the Baptist said something in John 3:30 that I've underlined in almost every Bible I have. It's something you should underline too. "He must become greater; I must become less." Some translations say, "He must increase and I must decrease."

This is the best way for a Christian to live. When we start to live like it's our power, our anointing, and our abilities that are accomplishing all this, He will remove that from our lives to reveal the truth.

We are nothing without Him! But *with* Him, we are more than conquerors. When Jesus gets the glory, He is in His rightful place and we are in ours. His glory goes up and our glory goes down. His glory exalts and magnifies him, and it pushes us to the floor in reverence. God's glory declares our position.

God's glory also demonstrated His presence. In Exodus 13, Israel had just left Egypt after 400 years of slavery. To show that God was with them, He manifested himself as a pillar of cloud during the day to guide them and a pillar of fire at night to give them light, warmth, and protection. It never left them.

That representation of God's presence stayed with them and gave them comfort. They were exactly where they needed to be. The path ahead wasn't going to be easy. There were going to be a lot of unpredictable moments to get them from the Sinai Desert to the Promised Land.

They would have to contend with Pharaoh's army, crossing the Red Sea, wandering in the wilderness for forty years because of their lack of faith, giants, cities that had to be overtaken, changes in leadership, betrayal, the golden calf, Korah's rebellion, and so many other events before they were ready to receive God's promise and step with faith-filled eyes into the Promised Land. All the while, God's presence guided them and protected them. The cloud by day and the fire by night.

What a holy and amazing experience that must have been! This experience introduced the Jews to "shekinah glory." The word "shekinah" comes from a Hebrew word means "to dwell or to rest." That meant that God's glory was dwelling permanently among them. His glory rested with them.

In Exodus 24, there was such an unusual moment tucked away in the story of when God enters into a covenant with Israel at Mount Sinai. Exodus 24:9-11 says, "Moses and Aaron, Nadab and Abihu, and the seventy elders of Israel went up and saw the God of Israel. Under his feet was something like a pavement made of lapis lazuli, as bright blue as the sky. But God did not raise his hand against these leaders of the Israelites; they saw God, and they ate and drank." To have dinner in God's manifest presence...I can't even imagine what that would be like.

As we understand the weight of glory, we see in the Bible that: *God's glory changes you.* I don't believe anyone can say they were unchanged by being in the presence of God.

For some of you, that moment was when you were baptized in the Holy Spirit. You felt God doing something totally unique in your life and it changed you. It changed the way you pray, it changed the way you feel God's presence, and the Spirit began to impart spiritual gifts in your life that weren't there before.

In Exodus 34, God gives Moses the Ten Commandments as he established his covenant and rule of law with the people. Exodus 34:29-35 states:

When Moses came down from Mount Sinai with the two tablets of the covenant law in his hands, he was not aware that his face was radiant because he had spoken with the Lord. When Aaron and all the Israelites saw Moses, his face was radiant, and they were afraid to come near him. But Moses called to them; so Aaron and all the leaders of the community came back to him, and he spoke to them. Afterward all the Israelites came near him, and he gave them all the commands the Lord had given him on Mount Sinai. When Moses finished speaking to them, he put a veil over his face. But whenever he entered the Lord's presence to speak with him, he removed the veil until he came out. And when he came out and told the Israelites what he had been commanded, they saw that his face was radiant. Then Moses would put the veil back over his face until he went in to speak with the Lord.

The presence of God had a physical effect on Moses. The people could not look at him because his face was shining so brightly. He spoke face-to-face with the living God and it changed him. This physical manifestation was something that Moses didn't even realize had happened and there was no way he could fabricate it.

This passage leads to my next point: *God's glory cannot be manufactured or faked.* In Pentecostal churches, we have seen things that didn't sit right. One time, I was at the altar in a youth service. A pastor put his hand on top of my head and pushed it backwards while his wife was behind me with her hands on my lower back pushing the other direction. I was being bent in half! Basically, I was going to the floor whether I wanted to or not.

That experience was *not* the work of the Holy Spirit; that was the work of flesh masquerading as the Spirit. I understand ministers get amped up and energetic. Pentecostal churches need a sign in the altar area that says "no pushing required." When the Holy Spirit comes upon you, no one has to even touch you.

I have seen God's glory come upon a teenager and he smacked his forehead down on the wooden platform step so hard it rattled *my* teeth. I thought he was going to get up with an insane headache, but he didn't. It was genuine and the Holy Spirit protected him from injury. I have seen people fall backwards and hit the back of their head on the edge of a wooden pew. If it was fake, they would've been knocked unconscious. But it was genuine and they were perfectly fine when they got up.

Non-Pentecostals are wary of manifestations of the Spirit because the abuses of it are all over YouTube. If you are a Pentecostal, I believe that you need to be quick to interject when people bad mouth the genuine working and moving of the Holy Spirit.

However, there are critics because there are abuses. In Leviticus 10:1-3, we see a perfect example of the abuse of God's glory. It says, "Aaron's sons Nadab and Abihu [the same guys who had dinner in God's presence in Exodus 24:11] took their censers, put fire in them and added incense; and they offered unauthorized fire before the Lord, contrary to his command. So fire came out from the presence of the Lord and consumed them, and they died before the Lord."

We're not entirely sure what "unauthorized fire" means, but we know this: (1) they knew what God required and (2) they knew they were doing something unauthorized, unholy, and manmade. They were willing to fake a requirement and fake their relationship with God. They had gotten comfortable being around God's presence and they took it for granted.

God demonstrated in that moment that His glory and His presence is not something we can manufacture. It isn't based on a decibel level. It isn't based on how enthusiastic a preacher is. It isn't based on any human effort. It *is* God's sovereign choice when, where, and how He manifests His glory to His people.

The next thing to understand is: *God's glory demonstrated His approval.* Because He sovereignly chooses to manifest His glory in certain ways at certain times, we see that His presence is a mark of approval and blessing upon a person or a gathering.

One Sunday at church, I felt God's presence in our service very powerfully. God was doing something in our midst. He did so because we magnified Him. We did not make it about us; we made it all about exalting Jesus. When we do that, He will fill up this place with His presence.

In 2 Chronicles 5, Solomon and his workers completed construction on the first permanent home for the Ark of the Covenant. Previously, it was housed in a Tabernacle made of curtains. But David wanted to build a Temple for God so he got all the materials ready and his son, Solomon, constructed it.

What a moment that must have been for the people! Solomon gathered all the leaders together in Jerusalem for the temple's dedication. They brought the Ark of the Covenant through the city, up the Temple steps, and into the Temple. The priests put the Ark down beneath golden wings of angels.

The priests stepped back out of the Holy Place in the Temple and they began to fill the place with the sounds of worship and adoration to God. One hundred and twenty priests sounded shofars; they all joined in unison to give praise and thanks to God for His presence and blessing on His people. They sang out: "He is good; His love endures forever." At the end of 2 Chronicles 5, it says in verses 13-14, "...Then the temple of the Lord was filled with the cloud, and the priests could not perform their service because of the cloud, for the glory of the Lord filled the temple of God."

Can you just imagine being literally pushed out of church by the presence of God in the place–having to worship Him in the parking lot because His glory was so thick? Sadly, most churches today wouldn't know the glory of the Lord because they've never felt it in their midst. Like it was in 1 Samuel 4, the glory has departed. God's presence no longer dwells there. Let that never be said of us!

My last point is this: *God's glory is why we live.* Isaiah 43:7 says that we were created for His glory. NASA has sent radio satellites out into space and discovered that every planet sings.[1] Every planet reverberates sound into space that, previously, only God could hear. Birds, dolphins, and every animal has a means of communication designed by our Creator. So it is with us. *Our lives are songs that we sing back to God, proclaiming his wonder, majesty, and glory to the earth.*

When Jesus was told that his friend Lazarus was extremely ill in John 11, it says in verse 4, "When Jesus heard this, Jesus said, 'This sickness will not end in death. No, it is for God's glory so that God's Son may be glorified through it.'" Lazarus did die, but Jesus showed up after he was dead for 4 days and raised him to life. Jesus performed miracles to bring glory to the Father. Bringing glory to God is why we live.

I want to conclude this chapter by sharing a passage of Scripture. Moses had climbed up on Mount Sinai getting God's instructions for the laws the Israelites would need to abide by, the instructions for building the Tabernacle, and a lot of other things. God gave Moses the Ten Commandments that were written in stone by the finger of God.

Moses came down to show the people what God had given them and he saw them dancing around a golden calf. He was furious and threw the Ten Commandments down, breaking them into pieces symbolic of the people breaking God's commands. When God threatened to destroy these idolatrous people, Moses defended the people to God asking Him not to destroy them for their sins. Leading this nation left him worn out from the burden of leadership.

Moses said to the Lord, "You have been telling me, 'Lead these people,' but you have not let me know whom you will send with me. You have said, 'I know you by name and you have found favor with me.' If you are pleased with me, teach me your ways so I may know you and continue to find favor with you. Remember that this nation is your people." The Lord replied, "My presence will go with you, and I will give you rest." Then Moses said to him, "If your presence does not go with us, do not send us up from here. How will anyone know that you are pleased with me and with your people unless you go with us? What else will distinguish me and your people from all the other people on the face of the earth?" And the Lord said to Moses, "I will do the very thing you have asked, because I am pleased with you and I know you by name." Then Moses said, "Now show me your glory." And the Lord said, "I will cause all my goodness to pass in front of you, and I will proclaim my name, the LORD, in your presence. I will have mercy on whom I will have mercy, and I will have compassion on whom I will have compassion. But," he said, "you cannot see my face, for no one may see me and live." Then the Lord said, "There is a place near me where you may stand on a rock. When my glory passes by, I will put you in a cleft of the rock and cover you with my hand until I have passed by. Then I will remove my hand and you will see my back; but my face must not be seen." (Exodus 33:12-23)

Moses was a bold man. He had spent forty days with God on the mountain but had never seen his face. It was like I described at the beginning where you're looking at a negative image and you can't make out details. At this point in history, he was at a place of frustration and exhaustion, both mentally and emotionally. His cry was, "God, I have seen the pillar of cloud and the pillar of fire. I have heard Your voice. I have seen Your hand carve out and write the Ten Commandments. But if I could just see Your glory; if I could just see Your face; if I could just look into Your eyes and have a revelation of You, I can get through this. I want to see Your glory!"

We can have good church services or we can have *God services*. Good services make us feel better about ourselves; they make us walk away feeling encouraged and in a good mood. There's nothing wrong with that. However, *God services* make us walk away feeling empowered by the Holy Spirit and ready to impact our world for God's kingdom.

I've had plenty of good services in my life. I want *God services*! I want to feel the presence of God in such a powerful way that we know God is in our midst, that lives are changed, marriages are healed, bodies are made whole, prodigals return to the Father, and God is glorified. I can't manifest that. The worship team can't play music in a specific way that manufactures it. It's a holy moment with God.

It takes us putting aside all the things we think we need to do and just seek His face. Would you just take a few moments today and let your heart cry out as Moses did, "Lord, show us your glory! We want to walk in your power! We want to walk in your anointing! We want to feel your presence! As we make our lives living testimonies of your grace and mercy, may we glorify and magnify and exalt Your name!"

5

The Weight of Silence

Before I begin, I want to give you a disclaimer. This is the one chapter in this book I've struggled with the most. I know I must be obedient to the Lord's direction, but this chapter may be harder to read than the other ones. I'm addressing the real and pressing issue of injustice and the church's response. I'm not candy coating this topic. For some people, this is, quite literally, a life or death issue.

Let's begin with a news report from September 15, 2017 out of South Sacramento, California.[1] I'm going to spare you the worst of the details, but you still won't like this story.

A woman asked her ex-boyfriend, Deandre Cheney, Jr. to watch her children while she took her brother to work. She was gone for forty minutes. In the time she was gone, her son, eight-year-old Dante Daniels, was killed by the man. Dante died trying to protect his seven-year-old sister as Chaney, a violent two-strike felon and registered sex offender, molested the girl.

The mother came home to the sounds of one of her children crying. She entered the home and walked towards the bedrooms when she was hit in the back of the head with a hammer and tied up. Cheney was in the process of dousing the house in lighter fluid. The mother was able to get out of the house and get to a neighbor to call the police.

Eight-year-old Dante had stepped in to protect his little sister, and was beaten to death with a hammer. He never made it to his second day of third grade.

I read this story and it has bothered me ever since. My heart broke for this little boy who did all he could to protect his little sister. I don't understand this kind of evil. And I have wrestled with how to respond to it.

Lest we think that this story is some sort of aberration, that this kind of horrific event is a rare occurrence, here are the facts: state agencies estimate that no less than four to seven children a day die as a result of maltreatment or neglect.[2] Eighty percent of the children that died from maltreatment or neglect weren't even old enough for kindergarten. In the vast majority of those cases, the abuser was a parent.

This would be a never-ending chapter if I told you the statistics about spousal abuse, the abuse of the elderly or mentally handicapped, or all the other abuses and injustices committed against people. We can all agree that any of these is unacceptable. Abuse of any kind is a violation of criminal law, but also of God's laws of how we are to treat one another.

When injustices and horrific things like this happen in *our* community, what do we do? What should our response be? What does God expect us to do? There are plenty of stories to choose from in the Bible, but we're going to look at one that gives us a good blueprint to follow.

The story of Esther begins with the story of a Persian king named Xerxes I. If you have ever heard of the three hundred Spartans that fought against Xerxes at the Hot Gates to keep him from enslaving Sparta, this may have been the same King. One of his wives displeased him so he put on a beauty pageant to determine who her replacement would be. Esther won this contest and God established her as the new Queen of Persia. She went from being a nobody to the most powerful woman in the world. Though she was Jewish, she kept her nationality a secret.

One of Xerxes's leaders, a man named Haman, was honored by the King and paraded through town. Everyone bowed down to him except Esther's older cousin, Mordecai, who had raised Esther as though she were his own daughter. This behavior by Mordecai was seen as blatant disrespect and enraged Haman. He found out that Mordecai was part of the Jewish people that had been exiled to Persia and decided to kill all the Jews.

Then Haman said to King Xerxes, "There is a certain people dispersed and scattered among the peoples in all the provinces of your kingdom whose customs are different from those of all other people and who do not obey the king's laws; it is not in the king's best interest to tolerate them. If it pleases the king, let a decree be issued to destroy them, and I will put 10,000 talents of silver into the royal treasury for the men who carry out this business." (Esther 3:8-9)

The declaration went out across the land and Mordecai heard about it. He wept as he realized that every man, woman, boy, and girl–his entire race of people–was about to be annihilated. He sent word to Queen Esther about the plot and urged her to go into the King's presence to plead for mercy and to put a stop to this plan.

She sent back word to Mordecai that if she appeared before the King without being summoned, she could be killed. Additionally, it had been more than a month since the King had summoned her. Mordecai replied with the most famous passage in this book.

When Esther's words were reported to Mordecai, he sent back this answer, "Do not think because you are in the king's house you alone of all the Jews will escape. For if you remain silent at this time, relief and deliverance for the Jews will arise from another place, but you and your father's family will perish. And who knows but that you have come to royal position *for such a time as this*?" Then Esther sent this reply to Mordecai: "Go, gather together all the Jews who are in Susa, and fast for me. Do not eat or drink for three days, night or day. I, and my maids, will fast as you do. When this is done, I will go to the king, even though it is against the law. And if I perish, I perish." (Esther 4:12-16, emphasis mine)

The first lesson we learn from Esther in combating the weight of silence is: *Stand up.* When she faced the reality that Jews in every part of Persia would be murdered, she had a choice to make. Mordecai reminded her that if she didn't stand up now, she would regret it for the rest of her life. If her nationality was discovered, her life wouldn't last long either. When the reality of the moment hit her, she knew she must do something.

Indifference and silence when we see injustice–especially from the church–isn't an appropriate response either. Deuteronomy 10:18 says God defends the cause of the orphan and widow. Psalm 68:5 says that God, in His holy dwelling, is a father to the orphan and defender of widows. God loves these people and He cares about them when society stops caring about them, when society has become indifferent to them, and when people stop remembering the names of victims.

Loving your neighbor is not a passive act. Love is active. Love serves, love provides, love defends, and love protects. How can we say we love our neighbor when we don't actively love them? How can we say we love our neighbor if we won't stand up for them, defend them, and help them?

Imagine God announcing to all the host of heaven that He was tired of the spiritual death and imprisonment of humanity. He wanted to send someone to save them from their sins and to bring them back into fellowship with God. As the Father looked all over heaven, His eyes rested on Jesus sitting on His throne. The Father hoped Jesus would stand up and say, "I will go! I will give my life for them! I will stand in the gap!" But instead, Jesus sat there and said, "No, I'm good. Someone else can do it."

That sounds ridiculous, but that's exactly what Christians across this country do on a daily basis when there is injustice. They are silent and they communicate to the world that God is silent too.

Dante Daniels had no hope of winning a fight against a 23-year-old man with a hammer. But what if Dante had an older brother? What if his dad had been home? What if Dante had someone in his life that would have stood up to the injustice and violence? Then there would be a very different ending to this story. But there wasn't. There wasn't anyone to protect that little boy or his sister from violent abuse.

One of the ways you can stand up for victims is to be their advocate to God. Pray for them, pray for God to heal their wounds, pray for their protection, and that evil wouldn't win the day.

There is a song called "Hosanna" that Hillsong Church sings. Part of the songs says, "...open up my eyes to the things unseen; show me how to love like you have loved me; break my heart for what breaks yours..." As God breaks our heart with what breaks His, we will get a passion to protect the defenseless–that their cause becomes our cause, because it's something that God cares deeply about.

The second way to avoid the weight of silence is to *speak out*. In Esther chapter 5, she did something that could have gotten her killed. She went before the King without being summoned. But the fasting and prayer of God's people and God's existing favor on Esther, caused the King to act favorably towards her.

He extended his golden scepter to her which meant that she was welcome in his presence. In fact, God had given her so much favor with Xerxes, that he told her in Esther 5:3 that he would give her up to half of his entire kingdom.

She used her moment to invite the King and Haman to a banquet in their honor. They went and had a great time. At the end of the banquet, Xerxes asked her again what it was that she wanted. She said she wanted them both to come to a banquet again the next night in their honor. They agreed, but Haman saw Mordecai on his way home and Mordecai still didn't bow down and honor Haman. That night, Haman commissioned a gallows seventy-five feet tall on which to hang Mordecai.

On the same night, the King couldn't sleep so he had them bring in some books regarding recent events to be read to him. One of the stories was about how Mordecai had stopped a plot to assassinate the King, but he had never been honored or rewarded for it. Xerxes called out to Haman and asked him how he would honor a man whom the King wanted to honor. Haman presumed the King was talking about himself, so he told him that such a man should have the King's robe placed on him, ride in the

King's chariot around town, and have someone shout from the chariot, "This is what is done for the man the King delights to honor!"

Then Xerxes said, "That sounds great! Go do that for Mordecai!" As I am sure you can imagine, this absolutely infuriated Haman, but he obeyed the King's command. Later that night, the King and Haman attended Esther's second banquet. While they were having a great time, Xerxes asked her again, "Queen Esther, what is your request? Up to half of the Kingdom of Persia will be given to you, if that's what you want."

In Esther 7, she finally told him what she wanted. She said, "If it pleases you, your majesty, grant me my life and the lives of my people. We have been sold for destruction and slaughter and annihilation." Xerxes responded by asking, "What man would dare do such a thing?" When he discovered it was Haman, they all knew his fate. But then someone said, "A gallows seventy-five feet tall has been built at Haman's house. He made it for Mordecai, the man who saved the King's life from assassination." The King immediately replied, "Hang him on it!"

What a different world we would live in if Esther had kept quiet! Think about the lives that were saved during the Holocaust by people who stood up to tyranny and injustice, and who spoke out against it. God will do his part! But He also expects us to do our part. He expects us to be the voice for those who do not have one– to speak on their behalf so that someone hears. The average of four to seven children dying a day from neglect and abuse is four to seven too many!

In America today, people make all sorts of excuses to be apathetic towards these issues. I have meetings; I have kids; I have time-consuming hobbies; I have Netflix to watch; I have parties to attend…Hey, we all have a million excuses not to step out of our comfort zone and speak up for someone in need! But if not us, then who? And if not now, then when?

If we say we're Christians, but don't live the way Christ called us to live, then what kind of Christians are we? If we say we're Christians and we come to church so we don't have to do anything outside of church, we're wrong. God has given us plenty of examples in Scripture to follow and He expects us to stand up and speak out.

He also expects us to: *Show up.* In America, it seems we would rather give money to a problem than to actually get involved with that problem. We feel like we can mentally and spiritually check off a box on our "Good-o-meter" that we've done something good for the week and we go on about our lives. Don't misunderstand me, giving donations to ministries is great and they depend on it. But instead of just donating, donate your money *and* your time. Show up and help.

Paul wrote in Romans 12 a discourse on what love in action looks like. He wrote in verses 9-16:

> Love must be sincere. Hate what is evil; cling to what is good. Be devoted to one another in brotherly love. Honor one another above yourselves. Never be lacking in zeal, but keep your spiritual fervor, serving the Lord. Be joyful in hope, patient in affliction, faithful in prayer. Share with God's people who are in need. Practice hospitality. Bless those who persecute you; bless and do not curse. Rejoice with those who rejoice; mourn with

those who mourn. Live in harmony with one another. Do not be proud, but be willing to associate with people of low position. Do not be conceited.

Then he wrote in Romans 12:21, "Do not be overcome with evil, but overcome evil with good."

The Irish statesman, Edmund Burke, said, "The only thing necessary for the triumph of evil is for good men to do nothing." We are God's hands and feet. While our main mission is to preach the gospel and make disciples, ministering to people's felt needs makes them open and receptive to the gospel. Hearing about a God who cares by seeing a Christian who cares opens them up to receive a Savior that cares.

Edmund Burke also said, "Nobody made a greater mistake than he who did nothing because he could only do a little." Mother Teresa echoed this statement and said, "If you can't feed one hundred people, then just feed one." Jesus said in Mark 9:41 that just by giving a cup of cold water to someone in need in His name would be rewarded.

In Matthew 25, Jesus told the story of the final judgment where God will separate the righteous from the unrighteous.

"Then the King will say to those on his right, 'Come, you who are blessed by my Father; take your inheritance, the kingdom prepared for you since the creation of the world. For I was hungry and you gave me something to eat, I was thirsty and you gave me something to drink, I was a stranger and you invited me in, I needed clothes and you clothed me, I was sick and you looked after me, I was in prison and you came to visit me.' Then the righteous will answer him, 'Lord, when did we see you hungry and feed you, or thirsty and give you something to drink? When did we see you a stranger and invite you in, or needing clothes and clothe you? When did we see you sick or in prison and go visit you?' Then the King will reply, 'I tell you the truth, whatever you did for one of the least of these brothers of mine, you did for me.'" (Matthew 25:34-40)

Stand up, speak out, show up, and finally: *Shine bright*. Jesus said in John 8:12 that He is the light of the world. But because we have accepted Jesus as our Lord and Savior and we are His ambassadors in this world, Jesus also said in Matthew 5:14-16, "You are the light of the world. A town built on a hill cannot be hidden. Neither do people light a lamp and put it under a bowl. Instead they put it on its stand, and it gives light to everyone in the house. In the same way, let your light shine before others, that they may see your good deeds and glorify your Father in heaven."

Key in on that last sentence because I think that is where some people get confused. It doesn't say people will see your Jesus sticker on your car and glorify your Father in heaven. It doesn't say people will see your smile, your house, your car, your blessings, or anything like that. It says they will see your *good deeds* and when they see your good deeds, it will cause them to glorify God.

In this day and age of selfishness, it's doing good when we don't have to that sets us apart. It's doing good in the name of Jesus that points people to this Savior that has changed us. We are surrounded by darkness and evil everywhere. We don't dispel darkness by selfishness or greed. We dispel darkness by being the light and shining that light. When we love people the way God has commanded us to, we are able to share the love of Jesus with them.

Jesus is the only way people will ever change. The gospel has transformed us and can transform anyone: hungry, thirsty, poor, or imprisoned. But how can they know of a God that loves them and died for them if no one is willing to go tell them?

We are God's greatest resource on this planet. He has blessed us with the ability to do good as His ambassadors so we have opportunities to love people the way God loves them and open up doors for sharing the gospel. He has blessed us with financial resources and supplies to donate and serve.

Knowing what God has called you to do and how God expects you to live, what are you going to do with that knowledge? We should go into the world, because He set the example by leaving His throne to come to us. We should love the unlovable because Christ loved us while we were still sinners.

We should give to those in need because Christ gave us something worth far more than anything money can buy. We should serve because Christ demonstrated true servanthood by laying down His life for us so that we would be reconciled to God.

I encourage you to Google a list of local places you can serve. There are ministries which reach out to meet people's felt needs. There are opportunities for you to shine brightly with the love of Christ. Ninety percent of the ministry of every church should be done outside of the church. God has blessed us to be a blessing to others, so he expects us to be just that. If we are unfaithful with the resources He has given to us, He will reallocate those resources to people who will be faithful.

Before you move onto the next chapter, would you just take a few moments and let your heart get a fresh revelation of the Father's love? Would you pray, "God, show me how to love like You have loved me. Break my heart with what breaks Yours. Open my eyes to the opportunities to shine Your love brightly on those around me. Let me see ways to serve and love all around me. Enable me to do good works so that people will glorify You and enter into relationship with You."

I believe we can change our community and the world by ending our silence and pursuing justice.

6

The Weight of Love

If you were to Google "songs with love in the title," you would find quite the variety and learn a lot about love from popular culture. You would learn that Celine Dion believes in "the power of love"; that Whitney Houston will "always love you"; that Beyoncé is "crazy in love"; that Robert Palmer is "addicted to love"; that Captain & Tennille believe love will keep them together; that Andy Williams believes "love is a many splendored thing"; or that Tina Turner asks, "What's love got to do, got to do with it?"

Our world loves to talk about love. Almost every book, TV show, and movie has a love interest or a love triangle where love creates tension among the characters. We talk about how much we love food, electronics, and people. Valentine's Day is great if you're in a relationship, but it can be very sad and lonely if you are not. Love is something that our culture really enjoys singing about, talking about, and entertaining us with.

Since each of these chapters has ended with a challenge in some way, the challenge today is this: *How do we love God and how do we love others?* This chapter will look at the life of King David to answer both of those questions because I believe they go hand in hand.

For those of you less familiar with David, he was the runt of the litter–the youngest boy of eight sons of a shepherd named Jesse. In fact, he was so small and insignificant in the eyes of his father and brothers, they didn't bother calling him into the house when the prophet of God was coming to anoint one of them as King over all of Israel. However, God wasn't looking at height or strength to determine who the next leader was; God was looking to see who had the right heart. David managed to fit that requirement perfectly.

David was a musician and worshipper. He had been called into King Saul's presence to play his harp and worship God, and it would provide comfort and peace to the King. Worship became the defining action of how David communicated his love for God. David was grateful to be chosen by God and anointed as the next King. He felt God's presence with him when he killed the bear, the lion, and Goliath.

When we ask ourselves: "How did David demonstrate his love for God?", the first way is simple: *Worship.* The word worship means to "kiss towards;" it's a term of intimacy. It's declaring that there's nothing more important in that moment than offering acts of love and affection to God. We don't sing worship songs on Sunday morning to fill time; we don't sing because we're showcasing talent; we sing because we love God and we long to declare our love and devotion to Him. David wrote in Psalm 86:5-10:

> You are forgiving and good, O Lord, abounding in love to all who call to you. Hear my prayer, O Lord; listen to my cry for mercy. In the day of my trouble I will call to you, for you will answer me. Among the gods there is none like you, O Lord; no deeds can compare with yours. All the nations you have made will come and worship before you, O Lord; they will bring glory to your name. For you are great and do marvelous deeds; you alone are God.

One day, all of the nations of the world will worship God. It is inevitable. The King of the Universe has saved us and made us His sons and daughters. With a loving Father like we have, how could we not worship Him? How could we stay silent? How could we keep our arms crossed and mouth closed when we see all that He's done for us?

Our worship is a love letter to God. We declare, "I love you Lord and I lift my voice to worship you." We sing, "Your love never fails, it never gives up, it never runs out on me"; "Amazing love, how can it be that You, my King, would die for me?"; "I could sing of your love forever"; "How deep the Father's love for us, how vast beyond all measure; that he would give his only Son to make a wretch His treasure"; "Love lifted me, love lifted me, when nothing else could help, love lifted me."

Some people don't sing during the worship time because they don't have any vocal ability. But that shouldn't keep you from having a heart of worship! If your lack of musical talent distracts your spouse or those around you, get away from everybody else if you have to. But don't lose an opportunity to bless God with your worship and to demonstrate your love for all that He has done for you.

Half of the Psalms in your Bible were written by King David. His heart was the heart of a worshipper. He didn't just worship when things were going great. So many of the psalms were written when he was being chased into caves by people trying to kill him. He learned how to worship God on the run!

He worshipped God after being anointed as King while Saul was still on the throne for years! He worshipped in the waiting. He worshipped in his frustration. He worshipped in his pain and loss. When everything was falling down all around him, when he was sick because of his sin, when his child died, when one of his sons stole his kingdom away from him–his response to all of this was to worship God!

There's never going to be an ideal time to worship. You'll feel sick; you'll feel tired; you'll be distracted; you'll be frustrated that someone parked in your parking spot or is sitting in your pew; you'll be focused on a bad diagnosis, a low bank balance, or a person who is trying to steal your joy. There are a hundred reasons why you don't feel like lifting your hands and worshipping God!

Yet you should lift your hands in worship because Jesus was lifted up for you on the cross. You should lift your voice in worship because Jesus spoke up and declared you righteous through His death. You should give every ounce of energy you have in worship because He gave every ounce of blood when He died on the cross. We don't worship because we feel like it; we worship because He's worthy of it!

When a worship album comes out by a group I like, I usually buy it and then listen to it non-stop. It drives my wife absolutely crazy. I'm not just listening to the songs; I'm learning the lyrics and the way they perform it. Years ago, I came across a song by Matt Redman called "You Never Let Go." No matter how many times I heard it, I didn't like it. In fact, the more I heard it, the less I liked it. The lyrics were fine, the music was okay. It was nothing spectacular. So every time it came to that song on the playlist, I would skip it.

Then I went through a prolonged period of unemployment. God had shelved me. I wasn't preaching anywhere. I wasn't involved in any ministries. God wasn't opening doors for me to use my gifts or abilities. I felt loneliness like I had never felt before. I felt like I was in a storm of unemployment and financial difficulty; I felt God wasn't answering my prayers like I wanted him to. Then I went to a church where they sang this song by Matt Redman.

As soon as the title came up on the screen, I just rolled my eyes. The worship leader began to sing the lyrics and the song became fresh and new to me. God began to break down all of my hurts, all of my frustrations, and all of my loneliness. The worship leader sang:

Even though I walk through the valley of the shadow of death, Your perfect love is casting out fear. Even when I'm caught in the middle of the storms of this life, I won't turn back; I know you are near. I will fear no evil. For my God is with me. And if my God is with me, whom then shall I fear? Whom then shall I fear? Oh no, You never let go, through the calm and through the storm. Oh no, You never let go in every high and every low. Oh no, You never let go. Lord, You never let go of me.

I wept. It was ugly crying. In all of the circumstances going on in my life, my *heart* overruled my *head* and said, "You are going to worship. Because of God's unfailing love, you are going to worship. Because of God's amazing grace, you are going to worship. Because of God's mercy and forgiveness, you are going to worship. Because you can't win this battle on your own, you are going to worship." The way we express our love to God is through worship.

In Micah chapter 6, God was frustrated with Israel's disobedience. They constantly fell into idol worship. God reminded them of all the things He had done for them. He brought to their remembrance all the times He saved them, fed them, blessed them, protected them, and delivered them from their enemies. Then the prophet Micah responded by writing in 6:6-8:

With what shall I come before the Lord and bow down before the exalted God? Shall I come before him with burnt offerings, with calves a year old? Will the Lord be pleased with thousands of rams, with ten thousand rivers of olive oil? Shall I offer my firstborn for my transgression, the fruit of my body for the sin of my soul? He has shown you, O mortal, what is good. And what does the Lord require of you? To act justly and to love mercy and to walk humbly with your God.

Micah said that God requires us to act with justice and mercy. It demonstrates our love for God, but also our love for others. I'm not talking about loving the people you already like. That's easy. Anybody can love a person that does nice things for them or acts generously. You can love those folks without breaking a sweat!

Love the people you *don't* like: the people who curse you, the people who betray you, the people who want to see you fail, the people that say your children are ugly, the people who are hoping your marriage falls apart, the people who steal from you, the people who wish you were dead.

Those people.

How do we love those people? Well, we don't *want* to! But we *have* to. I know firsthand what a battle it is just to not hate them. They've done something so horrible to you that your flesh wants to hate them, but your spirit knows that is wrong. So you compromise and tell God, "I can't love them, but I'll try not to hate them…as much."

There are some people that wound you so deeply that you will only be able to forgive them by the power of the Holy Spirit. In February 2018, the man who murdered my father on July 4, 2014 finally stood trial. I was there at the courthouse, sitting just a few feet away from him. So yes, I understand pain and loss and sadness caused by someone else.

There are two ways to demonstrate our love to others. The first is what the prophet Micah said: *Act justly and love mercy.* I know this man must stand trial for the crime he committed. The state requires justice be done. But through the power of the Holy Spirit, I have forgiven him for the crime he committed. Though his body belongs to the Department of Corrections, my prayer is that his soul belongs to Jesus.

It has taken me awhile to get to that point. You don't get healed of deep wounds overnight. It takes a whole lot of prayer and healing by the Holy Spirit to be able to forgive a murderer, someone who betrayed you, abused you, or hurt you deeply.

We love others by forgiving their sins against us the way God has forgiven our sins against Him. God so loved that He gave His Son and He so loved that He forgave.

The second way we demonstrate our love to others is: *Serve them.* I talked a lot about this in the last chapter, so I am not going to rehash that. But I challenged you to get connected with an organization or ministry that serves the community and get out there! You might already do and that is fantastic. I applaud your service and commitment. You might have meant to and I applaud your heart. Hopefully the previous chapter provided some motivation and you found a couple resources in the community to choose from.

When I look at the Bible, I see a book full of heroes. People who did impossible things that became possible through the power of the Holy Spirit. When I look at what the Apostles did in the early years of the Church after Jesus ascended into heaven, I'm just amazed at their accomplishments, their wisdom, their depth of theology and understanding of God's nature and work. These men were fearless leaders, great preachers, and were so powerfully used by God. Yet when they wrote letters to various churches, they didn't act like they were God's gift to the church. Instead, they focused on being a servant. Paul repeatedly identified himself as a servant of God and of people in his letters. James started his letter off by identifying himself as a servant. Peter did the same. Jude did that as well.

Every one of them highlighted their role in the body of Christ: no matter how big of a crowd they drew, no matter how famous they got, no matter how many churches they planted...it was all about being a servant. A servant of God and a servant to others.

As followers of Christ, we have to love like Jesus loved and serve like Jesus served. Start with the people in your home. Love them and serve them. Branch out to the people you work with and the people you see on a regular basis. Serve them and love them. Then branch out even further to the people that God leads you to. Serve them and love them.

As you do that, I believe something amazing will happen. I believe that God's love will abound in you as you worship God and serve others in love. It just may be that someone you come into contact with opens up their heart to you and is receptive to hear the gospel because of what you do.

Before you move on to the next chapter, I want you to ask God to give you a fresh revelation of His love. Ask God to open your eyes to the opportunities to love others in word and deed and that His love would flow out of you so effortlessly that people would see it and be drawn to a relationship with Jesus because of it. Pray that His love would abound in your heart and mind and that you would have a heart of worship to God and a heart of service to others. Make that your prayer today and every day.

7

The Weight of Discipleship

In a research study done just four years ago, seventy percent of all Americans identified themselves as Christians.[1] This doesn't mean that seventy percent of Americans go to church, read their Bible, pray, or do anything else. It just means that seventy percent of people identify themselves as Christian whether they accepted Jesus Christ or not, or even adhere to any of His teachings.

That's not good because people who say they are Christians do some very unchristian things. When they do, they give all the other Christians a bad name—even though most would never do some of those things or behave those ways.

Here are more alarming statistics: After one Christian concert, they followed-up with everyone who responded to the altar call. Less than five-percent said they were living a Christian life one year later.[2] After a mass crusade where 18,000 people accepted Christ, ninety-four-percent of them failed to get connected with a local church. When they surveyed over 11,000 churches in just one denomination, they reported almost 300,000 conversions, but almost ninety-five-percent of the new converts were not attending church.

The reason for this huge problem is simple: *churches across the nation emphasize conversions instead of discipleship*. Many churches provide nothing for Christians to use in order to grow spiritually and learn about the Bible. This leaves Christians spiritually malnourished and spiritually starving to death. They can't become disciples because they are saved, and then put back into an ungodly world with no training on how to overcome temptation or live like Christ. They aren't given a mentor or any tools to succeed. So it's no wonder why we have a large number of people who are Christians in name only and have never been discipled.

A disciple is defined as a person who accepts and assists in spreading the teachings of a person or movement. If you were to ask a person on the street what they think about Jesus, I think the vast majority of people–regardless of their religion–would at least say that Jesus was a great teacher, wise leader, and was an all-around great guy. Jews, Muslims, Hindus, and Buddhists would most likely all echo this.

While seventy percent of Americans claim to be Christians, ABC News stated that at least ninety five percent of Americans believe in God by some name.[3] This is what the Bible says about that: "You believe that there is one God. Good! Even the demons believe that–and shudder" (James 2:19). If belief in God isn't enough to redeem demons, it isn't enough to save anyone. It is the acceptance of Jesus's sacrificial death for our sins that saves us. Paul said in Ephesians 2:8, "For it is by grace that you are saved, through faith..." Faith is not a noun. It isn't something you either have or do not have. Faith is active.

We don't engage in discipleship activities *to be* saved; we do them *because we are* saved and we want to know Jesus more and more. James 2:17 says, "...faith by itself, if it is not accompanied by action, is dead." The New King James Version simply puts it: faith without works is dead. This means that once we accept Christ, we have to get busy learning more about Him, His teachings, and the requirements He laid out for belonging to Him. It isn't a passive behavior. Just like being physically healthy requires deliberate activity on your part with diet & exercise, to truly be a disciple of Jesus Christ requires activity as well.

There's a story in 2 Kings 7 about the siege of Samaria. The inhabitants of the city are starving to death and there are four lepers that are sitting outside the city gates. One of them turned to the others and said, "Look, if we stay in Samaria, we're going to starve like everyone else here. If we go down to the enemy's camp, they might have pity on us and give us some scraps of food. But *if we stay where we are, we're going to die*." (emphasis mine)

That phrase has stuck with me all my ministry. If we stay where we are spiritually, we're going to die. Stagnant water stinks. So do stagnant churches and so do stagnant Christians. We absolutely must move forward in our faith. We must stay active.

Any muscle you don't use for long periods of time goes into atrophy. Atrophy is the wasting away of a muscle. If you don't feed yourself spiritually, if you don't pray, read your Bible, serve, obey Jesus's teachings, and grow, you will waste away spiritually and become yet another statistic of a Christian in name only.

You will become just another dead Christian and your church will become just another dead church. Because "...If we stay where we are, we're going to die."

Let's look at Jesus's model for disciple-making that you can implement in your life, whether you need to be discipled or you are mature enough in your faith to make disciples.

The first part of Jesus' plan to make disciples is: *"Come and See."* When Jesus first encountered someone, He extended an invitation for them to be introduced to him and what he was doing. In John chapter 1, Jesus extended invitations to Philip and Nathanael to join his group of disciples.

Let's read the exchange in John 1:43-51:

The next day Jesus decided to leave for Galilee. Finding Philip, he said to him, "Follow me." Philip, like Andrew and Peter, was from the town of Bethsaida. Philip found Nathanael and told him, "We have found the one Moses wrote about in the Law, and about whom the prophets also wrote–Jesus of Nazareth, the son of Joseph." "Nazareth! Can anything good come from there?" Nathanael asked. "Come and see," said Philip. When Jesus saw Nathanael approaching, he said of him, "Here truly is an Israelite in whom there is no deceit." "How do you know me?" Nathanael asked. Jesus answered, "I saw you while you were still under the fig tree before Philip called you." Then Nathanael declared, "Rabbi, you are the Son of God; you are the king of Israel." Jesus said, "You believe because I told you I saw you under the fig tree. You will see greater things than that." He then added, "Very truly I tell you, you will see 'heaven open and the angels of God ascending and descending on the Son of Man.'"

When I was a kid, I didn't want to invite my friends to church. I was afraid they would visit a service when someone would start speaking in tongues and then look at me like I belonged to a cult. At that time, I didn't understand it because I hadn't been baptized in the Holy Spirit yet, so I couldn't explain it. I was afraid they would think I was crazy for going to a church like that.

As I grew up and experienced the beauty and power of the Holy Spirit, I wasn't ashamed of it and I wasn't afraid to invite people to my Pentecostal church. The move of the Spirit, the gifts of the Spirit, and the manifestations of the Spirit showed that our God was alive and well. He longed to speak to us, minister to us, and use us for His glory. It gave me opportunities to take my friends to the Book of Acts, show them that it is one hundred percent biblical, and lead them to a relationship with Jesus.

As we come in contact with people in the community, some may say they have never been to church before. That might surprise those of us who live in the so-called "Bible belt." Regardless of how many people self-identify as Christian, that doesn't mean they have ever accepted Christ as their Lord and Savior, ever read two sentences in the Bible, or ever stepped foot in a church. Sadly, this stage is where many Christians seem to be.

When you come in contact with people that are on your radar to witness to, one of the first things you can do is tell them, "Come and see." Engage with them, have meals with them, pray for them, talk about your faith, and let them see your faith in action. Bring them to church if they're ready, but more importantly, let them see Christ in you. You are the best advertisement for Christianity because Christ's love and message goes where you go. They need to come and see what a difference Christ has made in your life.

The second part of Jesus's plan to make disciples was: *"Come and Follow Me."* In Matthew 4, Jesus approached Peter, Andrew, James, and John telling them to follow him. They left their nets, their jobs, and their parents to follow Jesus. They didn't know where they were going, what they would do when they got there, or even who Jesus really was. Jesus invited them to see what He was up to. He had authority and something in these young men beckoned them to follow Jesus.

As they followed, they saw Jesus perform miracles, heal the sick, raise the dead, and feed thousands of people. Yet seeing this didn't make them followers. Lots of people saw the works of Jesus and didn't follow him.

To follow Him meant that a person accepted Jesus's training and was willing to be obedient to the commands He laid out. Following Jesus was then and is now a deeper level of devotion. It means a person spends time with Him in prayer and study of the word. It is an increased level of commitment. A person in this stage of discipleship is really learning what it means to be a Christian and how to follow Christ's commands. This is where maturity begins because this is where a real relationship with Jesus starts.

This is the stage that many born-again Christians are in and, sadly, get stuck in. They love Jesus and they love the stories of the miracles that He did. Jesus is the ideal that they know they should live up to. But many in this stage still struggle with temptation. They still struggle with doubts. Many can't manage to share their faith with others because they don't feel like they know enough or are strong enough to be a good example for someone else.

My dad used to say that the way you express love to someone else is to give them time. Everyone values their own time and how they spend it. They spend their time on things that are important to them and avoid wasting time on things unimportant to them. If you love something, you give it time.

If you are in this stage of discipleship–no matter how long you've been there–don't get discouraged. Give Jesus your time and I promise you will grow. Before you go to bed tonight, open your Bible and read at least one chapter. Start in the Gospel of Mark and start reading.

After you read, pray for at least 5 minutes. The first night, you might not think of a lot to say, but each night, you will be able to think of more things. Pray throughout the day–talk to God about what's going on in your life, your struggles, your temptations, your concerns, and ask God for help in these areas. Start praying for others. Pray for your spouse, or your future spouse if you are unmarried. Pray for unsaved loved ones. Pray that God uses you for His purposes and that He blesses you so you can be a blessing to someone else.

If you love Jesus, give that relationship your time. The more time you give it, the better relationship it will be, the more of Jesus you will exhibit to others, the more you will grow spiritually, and the more you will want to share God's love with those you come in contact with.

The last stage of Jesus' disciple-making model is: *"Come and abide with me."* This is the discipleship stage where Jesus spent His most precious time with the disciples. He pulled aside twelve men from the crowd and invested in them. Because of their proximity to Jesus, they saw things that other followers and disciples of Jesus didn't get to see. He took them on field trips. They saw Him perform miracles. They had a greater closeness to Jesus. He saw their potential and poured into them so that they could become the kind of men He believed they could be.

To abide means to remain, to dwell, to rest with, to sit down with, to gather together, to have conversation, or to continue being in the presence of someone. Jesus said in John 15:1-10 (NKJV):

"I am the true vine and my Father is the vinedresser. Every branch in me that does not bear fruit He takes away; and every branch that bears fruit He prunes, that it may bear more fruit. You are already clean because of the word which I have spoken to you. Abide in Me, and I in you. As the branch cannot bear fruit of itself, unless it abides in the vine, neither can you, unless you abide in Me. I am the vine, you are the branches. He who abides in Me, and I in him, bears much fruit; for without Me you can do nothing. If anyone does not abide in Me, he is cast out as a branch and is withered; and they gather them and throw them into the fire, and they are burned. If you abide in Me, and My words abide in you, you will ask what you desire, and it shall be done for you. By this My Father is glorified, that you bear much fruit; so you will be My disciples. As the Father loved Me, I also have loved you; abide in My love. If you keep My commandments, you will abide in my love, just as I have kept my Father's commandments and abide in His love."

There is a lot to unpack here, so let me use a visual representation of what Jesus is saying. Based on His analogy, visualize Jesus as a tree. The Father is the gardener that takes care of the tree and keeps it growing healthy. Jesus said that if there is a branch that is not bearing fruit, the Father "takes it away" or cuts it off completely. It has no use to the tree but is only sapping resources from the healthy branches.

However, if there is a branch that is fruitful, the Father prunes it by making it even more fruitful.

According to a study by the University of York in England, they found that when a plant is pruned, it releases a hormone to stimulate additional growth.[4] If a branch is completely cut off, that branch withers and dies. But when a branch is pruned, the hormone flows through the plant and gives new life and health to the plant. Pruning doesn't hurt the plant and it isn't done out of frustration. It's done because what is fruitful can become even more fruitful by this action of an effective gardener.

Jesus said in John 15:4, "Abide in me, and I in you. As the branch cannot bear fruit of itself, unless it abides in the vine, neither can you, unless you abide in me." The way this works in nature is that the tree has roots that are in soil. It processes the water up through the plant to give the necessary nutrients to the plant.

The branch doesn't bear fruit if it's cut off from the tree. Doing that cuts it off from its source of nutrients. If you cut a branch entirely off, it will wither up and die, yielding no more fruit. It can't do anything by itself. It must be connected to the tree to stay healthy and to do anything. If the branch stays connected to the tree, if it *abides*, then it will be fruitful. And if it is fruitful, the Father will ensure it has everything it needs to be even more fruitful than it was at the start.

Hopefully, you grasp the analogy Jesus was making, because Jesus then added something that is incredibly important. If we abide–if we remain in Him, if we stay close to Him, if we dwell in His presence, and stay connected to Him–He said in John 15:7-8, "…you will ask what you desire, and it will be done for you" and that "By this My father is glorified, that you bear much fruit."

Please understand this isn't license to ask Jesus for a Lamborghini, a bigger house, or anything like that. *If we abide in Jesus, we will want the things that He wants for us.* When we desire godly things, there is no reason for God to say no to that because those are His desires for us as well. If we love the things He loves, He will give us those things if we ask for them. Godly things bring glory to the Father and cause people to sit up and take notice.

For instance, let us say you prayed and God gave you a burden for orphans in Rwanda. You researched the needs of the children there. Your heart broke for the suffering they had endured and their immediate physical needs, but they also needed the gospel. You prayed even more and asked God, "How can I minister to them? Are you sending me?"

The more you prayed, the more burden you felt until you absolutely knew that God wanted you to become a missionary to the children of Rwanda. Your heart was filled with love for them and you wanted what God wanted for you because you were abiding in Him. You had fallen in love with something that God loves and so, yes, God gave you that desire because you heard His heart and you were willing to act on it.

That is abiding. That is a mark of spiritual maturity. You are fruitful and God begins to prune things from your life to make you even more fruitful for His kingdom. He does it because He loves you. He implants desires in your heart so that you want what God wants.

I don't know what stage of discipleship you find yourself in, but I know this: no matter where you are, there is always room for growth. Since the standard that was set is Jesus himself, there are always areas we can improve upon. There is always more to learn. There is always room for pruning and progress. The disciples spent three years going where Jesus went, hearing what He said, seeing what He did–and even they had to completely rely on the Holy Spirit to guide and direct them after Jesus ascended into Heaven.

There is never a day living on this earth where we will say, "I have arrived. I know enough. I have all of Jesus in my life and there is nothing more I could learn or no way I could grow anymore." We should always be growing in our relationship with Jesus because *if we stay where we are, we're going to die.* I want to know Him more and more. I want to be more like Him than ever before. I want to be more effective at sharing His love and the good news of Jesus with everyone I meet.

You may be in the *"Come and see"* stage where you are checking out what Christianity is all about. If that is you, then you will never have a better time to accept Jesus Christ as your Savior and Lord. That means that He saves you from your sins and He helps you live your life for Him. As Peter said in Acts 2:38, "Repent and be baptized–in Jesus's name–for the forgiveness of your sins." Repentance is not just saying you are sorry for what you have done. It means to turn from those things that are wrong and follow Jesus. Immerse yourself in Jesus. Dive in to this Christian life, talk to God by praying, learn more about God through reading the Bible and regularly attending church, and invest in your own spiritual development.

If you are in the *"Come and follow Me"* stage, then there are still some areas of your life that need to grow and develop. You have made the most important decision by accepting Jesus and choosing to follow Him. But there is still room for progress. There are still some areas of your life that you haven't surrendered to Jesus. Because of that, temptations and struggles still abound. Jesus doesn't want you to just follow Him, He wants you to go deeper and abide with Him.

Some of you may be in the *"Abide with Me"* stage with Jesus and that's awesome! If you are there, then you know it takes work and deliberate action on your part to stay connected with Jesus. Just like you can't ignore your spouse and expect to stay in a fully-functioning and happy marriage, you can't ignore your relationship with Jesus and expect to keep growing.

When I think of a fully-functioning disciple of Jesus Christ, it reminds me of the lyrics to the hymn, "I surrender all." Let that be your prayer, the cry of your heart. It says, "All to Jesus, I surrender. All to Him, I freely give." Don't just be a Christian, be a disciple. Don't just be a follower, continue to grow in Jesus and share that message with those around you.

GRAVITY

ABOUT THE AUTHOR

Jason M. Frazier is a husband, a father of five, an avid reader, and a follower of Jesus Christ. He is a former Officer in the US Army Reserve. He has been a credentialed minister since 1996.

He earned his undergraduate degree from Southwestern Assemblies of God University, his Master of Arts in Religion from Liberty University, and is currently working on his Doctorate (D.Min.).

He plays four instruments, has written over thirty poems, and actively follows Scottish and English Football.

He can be reached via e-mail at jmfrazier76@gmail.com

End Notes

Chapter 1
1. https://www.washingtonpost.com/archive/politi cs/1987/03/01/oral-roberts-starts-vigil-for-8-million/b5e4f503-af46-4244-a4d0-69e5b237c342/?utm_term=.88f300852d12

Chapter 2
1. http://www.thetravelingteam.org/stats/

Chapter 4
1. http://thespiritscience.net/2015/06/15/nasa-discovers-planets-and-stars-give-off-music-this-is-what-it-sounds-like/

Chapter 5
1. https://www.sacbee.com/news/local/crime/artic le173643211.html
2. https://www.childhelp.org/child-abuse-statistics/

Chapter 7
1. http://www.pewforum.org/2015/05/12/americas -changing-religious-landscape/
2. *"God Has a Wonderful Plan for Your Life*, by Ray Comfort, 1999
3. http://www.washingtonpost.com/wp-srv/politics/polls/wat/archive/wat042400.ht m?noredirect=on
4. https://www.york.ac.uk/news-and-events/news/2009/pruning-plants/

My Notes

GRAVITY

23308547R00081

Made in the USA
Lexington, KY
16 December 2018